Why Do Good People Suffer?

Published by:
Gita Publishing House
Sadhu Vaswani Mission,
10, Sadhu Vaswani Path,
Pune -411 001, (India).
gph@sadhuvaswani.org

Ninth Edition

ISBN : 978-93-80743-45-5

Printed by:
Mehta Offset Pvt. Ltd.
Mehta House,
A-16, Naraina Industrial Area II,
New Delhi- 110028, (India).
info@mehtaoffset.com

Why Do Good People Suffer?

J.P. VASWANI

GITA PUBLISHING HOUSE
PUNE, (INDIA).
www.dadavaswanisbooks.org

Other Books and Booklets by Dada J.P. Vaswani

In English:
10 Commandments of A Successful Marriage
108 Pearls of Practical Wisdom
108 Simple Prayers of A Simple Man
108 Thoughts on Success
114 Thoughts on Love
A Little Book of Life
A Simple And Easy Way To God
A Treasure of Quotes
Around The Camp Fire
Begin The Day With God
Bhagavad Gita in a Nutshell
Burn Anger Before Anger Burns You
Daily Inspiration
Daily Inspiration (Booklet)
Destination Happiness
Dewdrops of Love
Does God Have Favourites?
Ecstasy and Experiences
Formula For Prosperity
Gateways to Heaven
God In Quest of Man
Good Parenting
Gurukul
Gurukul II
How To Overcome Depression
I am a Sindhi
In 2012 All Will Be Well
Joy Peace Pills
Kill Fear Before Fear Kills You
Ladder of Abhyasa
Lessons Life Has Taught Me
Life After Death
Management Moment by Moment
Mantras For Peace Of Mind
Many Paths: One Goal
Nearer, My God, To Thee!
New Education Can Make the World New
Peace or Perish
Positive Power of Thanksgiving
Questions Answered
Sadhu Vaswani : His Life And Teachings
Saints For You and Me
Saints With A Difference
Secrets of Health And Happiness
Shake Hand With Life
Short Sketches of Saints Known & Unknown
Sketches of Saints Known & Unknown
Stop Complaining: Start Thanking!
Swallow Irritation Before Irritation Swallows You
Teachers are Sculptors
The Goal Of Life and How To Attain It
The Little Book of Freedom From Stress
The Little Book of Prayer
The Little Book of Service
The Little Book of Success
The Little Book of Wisdom
The Little Book of Yoga
The Magic of Forgiveness
The Perfect Relationship: Guru and Disciple
The Seven Commandments of the Bhagavad Gita
The Terror Within
The Way of Abhyasa (How To Meditate)
Thus Have I Been Taught
Tips For Teenagers
What You Would Like To know About Karma
What You Would Like To know About Hinduism
What To Do When Difficulties Strike
You Are Not Alone God Is With You!

Story Books:
101 Stories For You And Me
25 Stories For Children and also for Teens
It's All A Matter of Attitude
Snacks For The Soul
More Snacks For The Soul
Break The Habit
The Lord Provides
The Heart of a Mother
The King of Kings
The One Thing Needful
The Patience of Purna
The Power of Good Deeds
The Power of Thought
Trust Me All in All or Not at All
Whom Do You Love the Most
You Can Make A Difference

In Hindi:
Aalwar Santon Ki Mahan Gaathaayen
Atmik Jalpaan
Aapkay Karm, Aapkaa Bhaagy Banaatay Hein
Atmik Poshan
Bhakton Ki Uljhanon Kaa Saral Upaai
Bhale Logon Ke Saath Bura Kyon?
Dainik Prerna
Dar Se Mukti Paayen
Ishwar Tujhe Pranam
Jiski Jholi Mein Hain Pyaar
Krodh Ko Jalayen Swayam Ko Nahin
Laghu Kathayein
Mrutyu Hai Dwar... Phir Kya?
Nava Pushp (Bhajans In Hindi and Sindhi)
Prarthna ki Shakti
Pyar Ka Masiha
Sadhu Vaswani: Unkaa Jeevan Aur Shikshaayen
Safal Vivah Ke Dus Rahasya
Santon Ki Leela
Sri Bhagavad Gita: Gaagar Mein Saagar

In Marathi:
Krodhala Shaanth Kara, Krodhane Ghala Ghalnya Purvee (Burn Anger Before Anger Burns You)
Jiski Jholi Mein Hain Pyaar
Life After Death
Pilgrim of Love
Sind and the Sindhis
Sufi Sant (Sufi Saints of East and West)
What You Would Like To Know About Karma

Other Publications:

Recipe Books:
90 Vegetarian Sindhi Recipes
Di-li-cious Vegetarian Recipes
Simply Vegetarian

Books on Dada J. P. Vaswani:
A Pilgrim of Love
Dada J.P. Vaswani: His Life and Teachings
Dada J.P. Vaswani's Historic Visit to Sind
Dost Thou Keep Memory
How To Embrace Pain
Living Legend
Moments with a Master

Publishers' Note

Why me?

This is the universal question that haunts most of us when faced with a seemingly unanswered problem or situation, or when we are struck with a long-suffering, incurable disease.

This beautifully illustrated book helps you just then. It contains a choice selection of Dada J.P. Vaswani's lectures and articles which will provide answers to several questions you always longed to know about suffering. The author, Dada J.P. Vaswani is a multi-faceted diamond, shining with an unearthly, resplendent light. His words have the power to ennoble, enrich and elevate, for they flow spontaneously from his love-filled heart.

A challenging book, which will open for you new insights into the law of *karma* and reincarnation. It gives these most profound philosophies in a language all can understand. In it are given practical guidelines for a radiant, joyful, God-filled life!

CONTENTS

Why Do Good People Suffer?

The topic for this evening's talk is, "Why Do Good People Suffer?" The very fact that so many people have gathered here today is sufficient proof of our interest in the subject. Almost at every place where I go, in India or abroad, people put to me the question: "Why do good people suffer?"

The story is almost the same every where. The people say: "We have been honest and hard working: we have not hurt or exploited anyone: we have done as much good as we could: and yet we have had to suffer. What is the reason?"

I am reminded of a young man. He built up a flourishing business in Bombay. Then he turned his attention to spiritual things. He, as it were, handed over his business to assistants whom he trusted implicitly. They proved to be dishonest. Very soon, this young man found himself in a difficult situation. He was on the verge of bankruptcy. Winding up his business, he went to America where he opened a shop. Misfortune dogged his footsteps. One afternoon, two black men entered his shop with pistols in their hands. One of them caught hold of him and said: "If you stir or utter a word, you will not be alive!" The other ransacked the shop and filled the booty in a waiting van and, before any action could be taken, the two quickly vanished.

In the course of a letter, this young man wrote to me: "Why did this happen to me? I pray many times everyday. I seek God's help and protection. Every morning, as I get up, I offer a prayer: I Spend some time in quiet meditation. Before I open the shop, I pray. Throughout the day, I keep thinking of God and offer small prayers to Him. I pray again at night, before I go to sleep. I have hurt no one: I have cheated no one. I have never been dishonest. Why, of all the people, did this happen to me?"

I think of a young woman. She stays in Singapore. She is God-fearing. She is an active member of a Yoga Society. Some months ago, she came to India, along with her family members. They visited a number of sacred shrines. They met holy men and sought their blessings. Then they returned to Singapore. A few days thereafter, their office premises were gutted by fire, and precious documents were destroyed. The girl, with tear-filled eyes, exclaimed: "Why is it that this happened to us? We visited India in a spirit of reverence, sought the blessings of a number of holy men and women. Why did this happen to us?"

I read concerning a woman. She went round the world collecting rare and precious antiques. After six laborious years, she returned to her country where she planned to start a business in antiques. A week before the inaugural function, a fire broke out and a number of shops, including her own, were destroyed. Her hard work of six long years proved futile. Her priceless collections, her irreplaceable curios, were reduced to ashes! No insurance claim could compensate her adequately. She put the same question: "Why did the All Merciful God permit this to happen to me?"

Let me tell you of yet another woman. She devoted the best part of her life to social service. She was, by nature, affable, amiable, energetic, vivacious. She went out of her way to bring joy and comfort into the lives of many. Suddenly, one day, she found herself losing her balance as she walked. A few days later, as she returned home, one night, she stumbled and fell across the threshold of her house. The next day, she was examined by a doctor, who, after a thorough check-up, diagnosed the disease as Multiple Sclerosis. She was told that it was a degenerative nerve disease which, with the passage of time, would gather momentum and restrict her mobility. Ultimately, she would not be able to walk without a support and would be confined to a wheel-chair. She might even lose bowel and bladder control and be dependent on others for her routine chores. This lady, too, could not understand why this had happened to her when many of her friends lived normal, healthy lives. "Why did God permit this to happen to me?" she asked.

Some people believe that there are certain obligations they owe to God and, if they fail to fulfil them, they or their dear ones are punished. One such woman met me when I visited Ottawa, Canada. She told me that she recited the second, twelveth and the eighteenth chapters of the *Bhagavad Gita* every day, before taking her lunch. She observed, also, the *Satyanarayan* fast, every month. But, during a whole month, she missed out on the recitation and the fast. The day after *Satyanarayan*, her husband, who was perfectly healthy and normal, suffered a stroke, and has remained paralysed since then. The woman put to me the question that was uppermost in her mind: "Has this anything to do with my failure to read from the scriptures and observe the fast? Is there any cause and effect relationship between the two?"

I think of a young man. He was the only son of his parents, who are good and kind, and obliging by nature. With his pleasant manners, the young man easily won over the hearts of many who knew him. One night, the car in which he was returning home, collided against a truck, killing him and three of his other friends. When the news was conveyed to his parents, they cried: "Why did the Merciful Lord allow this to happen to us? Why was our only son snatched away from us?"

A learned Rabbi has written a book entitled *When Bad Things Happen to Good People.* In this book, the Rabbi narrates how his three-year-old son was afflicted with an incurable disease called Progeria. The effect of this disease, he was told, would be that the boy would not grow taller than three feet, would remain bald, and would age rapidly. Even as a child, he would have the appearance of an old man! Naturally, the father was grief–striken. "Why has God permitted an innocent child to become the victim of such a disease?" he asked. "He has hurt or harmed no one. Why has he been exposed to physical and psychological torture?" The author considers several similar cases and concludes that God is not omnipotent, as we believe Him to be. God has limited power. Within those limitations, God can exercise His discretion. But, there are forces over which He has no control. If those forces operate, God has no way of helping you out.

Dr. Annie Besant, the founder of the Theosophical Society, gave birth to a child who, during his infancy, suffered from convulsions. Suddenly the fever would shoot up and the infant would have a series of fits. The suffering of the infant was more than the mother could bear. She was at a total loss to understand how the All Loving, All Merciful, All Compassionate God had inflicted so much suffering on a harmless, guileless and perfectly innocent baby. She turned an agnostic and said that she was not sure if there was a God.

She worked on the staff of "The New Review". One day, she was asked to review *The Secret Doctrine* by Madame H.B. Blavatsky. As she went through this book, she came upon a chapter on *Karma and Reincarnation.* She read line after line of this chapter with deepening interest and a new awakening dawned on her. She began to understand that the present was not the only life that she or her child had lived; it was but one of the innumerable lives they had lived so far. The present life was but a fragment in the continuity of existence and, therefore, what an individual suffered today could be the product of what he (or she) had done in an earlier incarnation. The mystery was unravelled. Her entire attitude toward life changed.

The answer to the oft–repeated question, "Why do good people suffer?" becomes clear when we understand the operation of the law of *karma* and reincarnation. The law of *karma* is the law of cause and effect. Every effect must have a cause. The effect we see now must have a cause, recent or remote, Whatever happens to me today has a cause behind it.

Question: What is the concrete proof for this?

Dada: You will get concrete proof when you practise silence and enter the depths within you. The meaning of the mystery of the endless adventure of existence is there within you. As you enter into the depths within, the mystery is unravelled.

Question: Can you give us some concrete example?

Dada: An example has been given us in the *Mahabharata.* It concerns the blind king Dhritarashtra. After the *Mahabharata* war was over, Sri Krishna said to the Pandavas and Kauravas and all others: "It is time for me to return to Dwarka. But before I leave, tell me if there is anything I can do for you?" The blind king Dhritarashtra said to him: "I have been good to everyone: I have not been cruel or unjust to anyone. Why is it that I am blind and have lost all my hundred children?" And Sri Krishna said to him: "I would wish you get the answer for yourself. Meditate, go deep within yourself until you touch the astral self, and you will know!"

Dhritarashtra entered into deep meditation and contacted his astral self. The astral self keeps a record of our earlier incarnations. Dhritarashtra discovered that, in an earlier incarnation, he had been a tyrant king. One day, as he walked by a lake side, he saw a swan bird surrounded by a hundred signets. He asked his people to remove the eyes of the swan bird and kill all the hundred signets just to please his passing fancy! He then understood why he was blind and had to suffer the loss of this hundred sons.

Question: But isn't that a very lengthy process of

getting to know?

Dada: It is well worth it. You do not acquire a postgraduate degree overnight. You have to put in years of study. Just as there is the science of nature. So also there is the science of the spirit.

The Rishis of ancient India called it *Atmavidya*. *Vidya* means science. As natural sciences have their laws, so does *Atmavidya* – the science of the spirit – have its laws. One of those laws is the law of *karma,* another is the law of reincarnation.

Question: Dada, could you explain this law of *karma*?

Dada: The law of *karma,* simply stated, is the law of cause and effect. My beloved Master, Sadhu Vaswani, referred to the law of *karma* as the law of the seed. As you sow, so shall you reap. You cannot sow thorns and reap apples. The law of *karma* is universal in its application: it applies equally to all. We are sowing seeds everyday in the field of life. Every thought that I think, every word that I utter, every deed I perform, every emotion I arouse within me, every feeling, fancy, wish that awakens within me, are seeds I am sowing in the field of life. In due course, the seeds will germinate and grow into trees, and yield fruit – bitter or sweet – which I shall have to eat. No one else can do that for me. There are causes that produce their effects immediately. There are other causes that produce their effects after a long time. As an example, if you go to a party and overeat, it is a cause you have created. This cause produces an immediate effect, acute indigestion. There are other causes which take very long to produce their effect. But every cause must produce its effect, every seed must yield its fruit. This, in simple words, is the law of *Karma*.

We are told, all men are created equal. No one can be so blind or foolish as to imagine that there is actual equality of ability or environment or conditions of birth for all. Why, in the same family, all children do not have equality of ability or intelligence. There is a family of which the eldest son is an I.A.S. officer and the younger is unable to pass the S.S.C. Examination. We have a proverb in Sindhi which says: "The mother gives birth to children, each brings with himself his destiny." In other words, each one brings his *karma* with himself. There is a family of which the youngest son is a multimillionaire, while the eldest is so poor that he and his children are virtually starving, literally begging for food.

Two questions arise: 1) Is this inequality the result of *karma?* 2) And, if so, is it fair? The answer to both, as the great teachers of India have taught us, is in the affirmative. You are the architect of your own destiny. You are the builder of your own life. Every thought, emotion, wish, action creates *karma:* and we have been creating *karma* for thousands, perhaps millions of years. If our thoughts, emotions and actions are benevolent, so-called good *karma* results. If they are malevolent, evil or difficult, *karma* is created. The good or evil we generate attaches its effect to us and remains in our life-current until we have satisfied it by balancing it out.

Question: Why are our past *karmas* kept a secret from us?

Dada: Don't you think it is a great mercy of God

that our *karmic* links are not known to us? Else, it may be difficult for us to live in the world. Thus, for instance, there may be a man whose wife, in the present incarnation, was his bitter enemy in an earlier incarnation and has now become his wife only to settle previous accounts. If all this were revealed to us, what would be our condition?

Question: How did bad *karma* originate?

Dada: Man was given free will, he was given the right of choice. He can choose between what the *Upanishads* call *preya* and *shreya*. *Preya* is the pleasant: the path of *preya* is the path of pleasure that lures us but leads to our degradation. As a Danish proverb has it: "After pleasant scratching comes unpleasant smarting." *Shreya* is the good: the path of *shreya* may, at first, be difficult to tread but, ultimately leads to our betterment and well-being and spiritual unfoldment. At every step, man is given this choice. Many of us, alas, choose the easy path, the path of pleasure, and so keep on multiplying undesirable *karma*.

Question: If all that happens today is the result of our past *karmas,* does it mean that everything is predestined?

Dada: No, certainly not! We are the architects of our own destiny. We are the builders of our future. Many of us blame fate, *kismet* for our misfortune. But let me tell you, dear friends, that you are the builders of your own fate. Therefore, be careful especially of your thoughts. We pay scant attention to our thoughts, believing that they are of no consequence. We say, after all, it was only a thought, what does it matter? Every thought is a seed you are sowing in the field of life, and what you sow today, you will have to reap tomorrow.

God has created a universe of beauty, fullness, happiness and harmony. Each one of us is a child of God. God wishes each one of us to be happy, healthy, prosperous, successful and to enjoy all the good things He has created. We keep ourselves away from all those bounties because of our *karma*. Change your *karma* and you will change the conditions in which you live. And you can change your *karma* by adopting a new pattern of thinking.

Question: Dada, can *karmas* be wiped off by *japa*?

Dada: It is believed that the effects of *karma* can be mitigated through *nama japa*. In any case, the suffering can be reduced, because *nama japa* acts as a sort of chloroform. It is like going through an operation. The surgeon puts you under an anaesthetic and you come out of the operation without feeling acute pain. Else the pain is so excruciating that a person could die of it. This is what *nama japa* does to you.

Question: Can saints take over the *karma* of their disciples?

Dada: They can. However, normally, they do not wish to interfere with the law of *karma*. For they know that the law of *karma* is not punitive but reformative. The law of *karma* does not wish to punish us for what we may have done in the past. The law of *karma* wishes to reform us and so sends us experiences which may help in our spiritual advancement. It is true there have been cases when men of God have taken the *karmas* of their devotees upon themselves. It is like having birds released from their cages. A man may purchase the birds and set them free. Likewise, a man who is rich in the wealth of the Spirit may, if he so desires, pay for our *karma* and release us from the cage of *maya*.

Question: Dada, tell us how to face suffering?

Dada: If our attention is on sufferings, they get magnified beyond all proportions. In the midst of suffering, let us count our blessings. Usually, we suffer only in one area of our life. There are so many other things for which we should be grateful. Take a piece of paper and make a list of all the blessings you still have. There was a man who started from a scratch and built up a flourishing business and one day became bankrupt. The first thing he did was to take up a piece of paper and write down all the things he still possessed. He found, he still had a great deal to be thankful for. With gratitude in his heart, he started anew and built up a still larger business. If we count our blessings, our suffering recedes into the background.

In all conditions of life, let us thank the Lord. Let us make it a habit, to praise the Lord at every step in every round of life. Even in the midst of fear and frustration, worry and anxiety, depression and disappointment, let these words come out of the very depths of our hearts: "Thank You, God! Thank You, God!" and we will be filled with a peace that will amaze us. When we thank the Lord all the time, we build for ourselves a ladder of consciousness on which we can climb and touch the very pinnacle of peace.

Let me tell you the story of a woman. Her husband fell seriously ill. The doctors despaired of his condition and said he would not be able to last longer than six months. The woman had deep faith in God and started thanking the Lord a thousand times everyday. "Thank You, God! Thank You, God!" she prayed again and again. "Thank You, God for having healed my husband and made him whole." She continued to offer this prayer even though there was no sign of healing in sight. Strange enough, a few months later, when the husband went for a check-up, the doctors were amazed at his miraculous recovery. "A power, above and beyond ours, has been at work!" they exclaimed.

Whatever be the condition in which you find yourself, whatever be the suffering through which you pass, keep on thanking the Lord all the time. When you do so, your heart expands and you become receptive to the helpful and healing forces of God.

In every situation, do the very best you can and leave the result to the Lord. When Henry Ford was seventy-five years old, he was asked the secret of his success. He answered: "My life is built in these three rules. I do not eat too much, I do not worry too much and, if I do my best, I believe that what happens, happens for the best.

You Can't Get Away With Anything

I have received an anonymous letter written by someone who was present at the last meeting. In the course of the letter, he writes: "Your talk outlined no new approach to the problem: Why do good people suffer? Many intellectuals present were rather disappointed. You asked us to repeat with you the words, "Thank You, God!" which, too, was very frustrating. Is India entering the 21st century, or still looking back? When will blind faith be wiped off from the country?" So let me apologise, my friends. I am sorry to have disappointed some who came here on the last occasion. I trust, they are not present here this evening, else they may be in for another disappointment. I confess I am not a scholar. I am not qualified to give intellectual interpretations. I do but aspire to give life-interpretations. The law of *karma* is an eternal law: it is a universal law. It needs to be interpreted in a life-interpretation of this and other eternal laws.

I recall having read many years ago, concerning an eminent Confucian scholar. He was 80 years of age, and

it was believed that no one could equal him in China in learning and understanding. One day he learnt that far, far away, a new doctrine had sprung up that was profoundly deeper than his knowledge. This upset him. He lost his interest in life. He decided that the issue must be decided one way or the other. He undertook a long journey, traversed many miles and met the master of the New Zen School. He asked him to explain the new doctrine. In answer, the Buddhist monk said to him: "Venerated Sir, the doctrine we propagate is a very simple one. It can be summed up in one sentence: "To avoid doing evil, to do as much good as possible, this is the teaching of all the Buddhas."

On hearing this, the old Confucian scholar, flared up and said: "What do you mean? I have come here facing the danger and hazards of a long, perilous journey in spite of my advanced age. And you just quote a little jingle that every three year old child knows by heart! Are you mocking at me?" The Zen master very politely answered: "I am not mocking at you. But, please consider that though every three-year-old child knows these words by heart, yet even a man of eighty fails to live up to them!"

It is life that is needed, not doctrines, creeds or dogmas. Do we bear witness to the great teaching in deeds of daily living? I recall an incident in the life of the eldest of the Pandava brothers. As boys, they went to an *ashrama* and the very first teaching passed on to them by their guru was: "*Satyam vad Krodham maakuroo*!" which means "speak the truth and never get angry!"

The next day the teacher asked the Pandava brothers if they had learnt the lesson. All of them, except Yudhishtra, the eldest, said they had remembered the lesson. Yudhishtra said, "Sir, I have learnt only the first half of the lesson. The latter half I have not yet been able to learn!" So, the teacher very patiently made him repeat the words, *"Krodham maakuroo! Krodham maakuroo!"*

But again, on the following day, when the teacher asked his students if they had remembered the teaching, Yudhishtra said he had not been able to memorise the second half of the words: *"Krodham maakuroo! Krodham maakuroo!"*

This went on for a week. On the eighth day, when Yudhishtra insisted that he had not yet learnt the latter part of the teaching, the Guru lost his temper and shouted at him: "How can you be so stupid? Your younger brothers learnt the lesson on the very first day. Why is it that you cannot remember two simple words, *Krodham maakuroo?"*

Then it is that Yudhishtra clapped his hands in joy and said: "Sir, I can say now that I have learnt the lesson!"

"How is it that a moment ago, you could not recall the words, and now you assert that you have learnt them?" asked the Guru, greatly surprised.

Yudhishtra said: "The first half of the lesson was easy to remember, because I always speak the truth. The latter half, viz., never yield to anger, I could not be sure if I had mastered, unless someone got angry at me, and in return, I remained calm. Today, I found that in the face of anger I was unruffled and so I can truthfully say that

I have remembered the teaching."

Yes, it is life that is needed, not book-learning, nor intellectual or psychological interpretations. Our friend writes in his beautiful letter that there is exploitation everywhere: exploitation and social injustice, and suffering due to maladministration. I agree: but I go a step further. Exploitation and social injustice and suffering due to maladministration are due to the fact that we have not learnt to interpret the law of *karma* in our daily life. If we truly believed in the law of *karma,* there would be no exploitation, for the law of *karma* boldly declares: "He that exploits shall be exploited." If India is to be made new, what is needed is not new interpretations but translation of the teachings in our daily lives.

Only a few days ago, I visited a sick woman. She is not learned in the lore of books. She had severe back-ache, excruciating pain at the base of the spine. She could neither sit nor stand, neither bend nor walk. Despite it all, there was a smile on her face as she said to me: "I must have done something during one of my earlier births to deserve this condition. Perhaps, I have beaten someone on the back with a stick. God, save me from doing any evil." And if this is the prayer of every-one who believes in the law of *karma*: "God, save me from doing any evil!" And if this becomes the prayer of every man and woman in India, this ancient, unhappy land will become new and India will shine, once again, in the splendour of the new morning sun. The root of exploitation, social injustice and maladministration is in the thought: I will get away with it! Once I know that in this open universe I cannot get away with anything, I shall be careful to see that there is no evil in my thoughts and actions.

I do an evil deed in the dark of the night, I say to myself: "No one saw it: I shall get away with it!" The law of *karma* tells me: It is true, no one saw it. But the seed has entered the field of life. The field of life has registered it. And one day or the other, today, tomorrow or in a distant future, out of the seed will grow a tree whose fruit will have to be eaten by you! Therefore, beware! Take care! Live and move and do your daily work in the ever-living presence of God!

This was the teaching that was given to every student in ancient India. There is an oft-repeated story of a guru and two disciples who came to him seeking admission to the *ashrama*. The guru gives them a simple test. He passes on a coconut to each one of them and instructs them to break the coconut where no one may see them, and return with the broken pieces. One of the students enters a dark and solitary cave and, finding no one watching, breaks the coconut and within no time, returns with the pieces to the guru. The other student returns only after sunset and that, too, with the coconut intact. His friend says to him: "Why did you not accompany me? There were so many caves. I entered one of them. You could have entered another and broken the coconut. Nobody would have seen you." At this, the other friend replied: "I entered cave after cave, but wherever I went, just as I was about to break the coconut, I found that He was watching me. God was watching me! There was not a nook or a corner where God was not!"

How many of us live in this consciousness? This is an ancient interpretation on an ancient, eternal law. But how many live up to it?

The students of the St. Mira's Primary School recite a beautiful song in their sanctuary almost everyday:

Be careful little eyes what you see:
There's a Father up above,
Watching you in love,
So be careful little eyes what you see!

Be careful little ears what you hear:
There's a Father up above,
Watching you in love,
So be careful little ears what you hear!

Be careful little tongue what you speak:
There's a Father up above,
Watching you in love,
So be careful little tongue what you speak!

Be careful little hands what you do:
There's a Father up above,
Watching you in love,
So be careful little hands what you do!

Be careful little feet where you go:
There's a Father up above,
Watching you in love,
So be careful little feet where you go!

Be careful little mind what you think:
There's a Father up above,
Watching you in love,
So be careful little mind what you think!

Be careful little heart what you feel:
There's a Father up above,
Watching you in love,
So be careful little heart what you feel!

If only we lived in the thought that God is watching us, exploitation, social injustice and maladministration would be completely eradicated from the country.

Let me relate to you an incident from the life of a judge. He was an honest and God-fearing man. One day, he was offered a bribe of two hundred thousand rupees. It was a large amount and he succumbed to the temptation. However, his conscience kept pricking him all the time. It kept saying to him: "You have sold your soul for a mere two hundred thousand rupees!" Finally, unable to quieten his conscience, he went to the rich man's house and returned the entire amount to him, saying: "There's a Father up above, watching us with love, so our hands must not give or receive a bribe!" How many of us would do likewise?

Books, doctrines, philosophies, intellectual interpretations will not make us new. What is needed is a new heart. And the heart becomes new through practise of simple truths in a spirit of faith and love.

On the last occasion, we made an attempt to understand a little of the law of *karma.* It is built up of two natural, universal laws. The first is: As you think, so you become! If you think thoughts of purity, you will become pure. If you think of disease, your body will be diseased. Many years ago, when psychosomatic medicine did not exist, an experiment was conducted to see if there was any effect of thought on the human body. A number of prisoners, sentenced to capital punishment, were asked if they would co-operate and offer themselves

for experimentation. Some of them agreed. They were told that their backs would be slit. A blunt wooden knife was passed down their backs, over and over again and a liquid, that looked like blood was poured on them. When the prisoners found themselves in a pool of blood, they instantly collapsed! Great is the effect of thought on the body. As you think, so you become.

Let me narrate to you an amusing incident from my own life. This happened when I was a little boy. One night, as I returned home, I felt thirsty, I filled a glass of water. No sooner did I take a few sips, than I noticed something wriggling which looked like a snake in the water. The very thought that I had taken poisoned water, paralysed me completely. I dropped down on the floor, muttering: "I am dying! I am dying!" Members of the family rushed to find what the trouble was. One of them ran to fetch a doctor. Another asked, why I felt I was dying. In a frightened voice, I explained to him that I had taken water from a glass that had a snake in it! My younger brother went to investigate and found that what had appeared, in the dark, to be a snake, was actually a rubber string. The moment I heard those words, I jumped up, strong as ever. Thought has a great influence on the body. Therefore, take care of your thoughts.

The first natural law is: As you think, so you become! The second law is: "As you sow, so shall you reap!" These two laws together are called the law of *karma*. Therefore, always think good thoughts. Always do good actions. Serve, Love, Give! Give happiness to as many as you can: and happiness will come back to you. The law of *karma* tells us that we must not speak falsehood, we must not steal, we must not criticise another, we must not indulge in backbiting, we must not obtain anything by dishonest means, we must not deny a promotion which has been earned by another, we must not deny to another his wages, we must not cheat others. When we cheat others, we only cheat ourselves.

There is a story told us concerning a son-in-law, who was an architect. His father-in-law, a wealthy man purchased a plot of land on a hill and entrusted him with the task of constructing a beautiful bungalow there. The architect, a dishonest man by nature, felt that was the chance of his life! The temptation to make easy money, drove him to use sub-standard material. The cement as well as the steel he used were of poor quality. When the bungalow was ready, the father-in-law informed him that it was a gift from him to his daughter! The face of the son-in-law lost colour as he thought to himself: "I did not know I was cheating myself!" If we but understand this law and put it into practice in daily life, we would be a source of blessing to many.

Why do good men suffer? In truth, good men can never suffer. If a so-called good man suffers, it means that there is still a particle of evil lurking within him. A man suffers so that the evil may be transmuted into good. How does evil become good? How does gold get purified? By passing through fire! Even so, if there are some particles of evil in a good man, he must pass through the fire of suffering. What a beautiful idea this!

Significant are the words of Sadhu Vaswani: "Every great one of humanity has had to bear his cross. Krishna and Buddha and Jesus walked through the valley of the shadow of death. Who are we to say: We must escape sorrow, anguish, pain? We, too, must bear our cross, bear and bleed. And when we bleed, let us remember the Will of God is working through us: and through suffering and pain, God's Will is purifying us, preparing us for the vision of the One Lord of Life and Light and Love in all that is around us, above us, below us, within us. Suffering is the benediction which God pours upon His beloved children to whom He would reveal the meaning of His Infinite Mercy– reveal Himself, His Wisdom and His Love!" God has created a wonderful world. He wants each one of us to be happy, prosperous and successful and to enjoy all the good things with which the universe is filled. If I am not happy, prosperous and successful, I may be sure that I have broken some natural law either in the present or in an earlier incarnation. Nature does not have courts or judges or magistrates or policemen who will arrest you, when you infringe any of her laws. Nature works in a simple way. If your thoughts, words, actions are in obedience to the laws of nature, you may be sure of a happy and harmonious life, for nature is conquered by obedience to her laws.

Thoughts, as I have already said, are forces: thoughts are things. Every thought I think is a force I generate for my good or evil. Every thought survives and has a form and colour. The thought may have the form of an angel or a demon depending upon its contents. If I think a thought of peace, purity, prayer, love, joy, sympathy or service, it will stick to me wearing the form of an angel. If I think a thoughts of envy, jealousy, hatred, ill-will, resentment, greed, dishonesty, it will stick to me wearing the form of a demon. Each one of us has around him these forms, angelic or demoniac, depending upon the type of thoughts we think. Take care of your thoughts and desires, your impulses and ambitions, your feelings and fancies. With these you are building your own life. No one else is to blame for your present condition. You have built it with your own thoughts and desires generated in the near or distant past. The forces that are around you have magnetic power. They draw to themselves forms of a like nature. If we are surrounded by angelic forms, they draw to themselves more angels. If we are surrounded by demoniac forms, they attract to themselves many more demons. We have heard of physically weak people performing heroic deeds of valour far beyond their physical strength. I read concerning a mother who weighed only 41 kgs: in a moment of crisis, she lifted the wheel of an automobile beneath which her child had been caught. From where did she get all that strength? The seemingly impossible is accomplished when determination is accompanied by high purpose. Referring to Sir Gallahad, Tennyson says: "His strength was as the strength of ten, because his heart was pure!"

Conversely, low thoughts have an evil and disturbing effect. Sometimes, in a fit of temper, we do things of which we are not otherwise capable. Later, as we repent for our evil deeds, we exclaim: "Some devil must have tempted me!" May I tell you, friends, we are not *attacked* by these entities: we *attract* them to us!

Question: How may we live a life that may bear witness to the law of *karma* ?

Dada: So let me pass on to you a few practical suggestions.

The very first practical suggestion is: Always be aware of your thoughts. As you think, so you become. Everytime a thought approaches you, push it out of your mind. An effective way of pushing out a thought is to slap or pinch yourself the moment an undesirable thought enters your mind.

Prophet Muhammad said: "Temptation comes as a passer-by. It knocks on the door of the heart and wishes to be admitted as a guest. If you let it in, it will stay as a master!"

Also, keep on reminding yourself, even in the midst of work, that you are not the body nor the mind. You are not a creature of the flesh, a creature of the earth, earthy. You are That, the Absolute, the Eternal *Atman*. Always keep this thought uppermost in your mind and keep on telling yourself: "I am not this: I am That!"

Practical suggestion No. 2: As you sow, so shall you reap. Therefore, be aware of every little thing that you do. Everyday spend sometime in silence, preferably at the same time and at the same place. Sitting in silence, go over all that you did during the earlier twenty-four hours. It is helpful if you go over your actions in the reverse order, i.e. think first of what you did a little while ago, then of what you did a little while earlier, and so on. You will surely find that there were things which you did but, which you should not have done as there are things which you did not do but should have done – many errors of commission and omission. Repent for them all and pray to the Lord for wisdom and strength never to do similar things again.

Practical suggestion No. 3 is, take care of your *sanga*, the people with whom you associate. If you move in the company of holy ones, something of their holiness will penetrate your life and fill you with holy aspirations and vibrations. Hence the value of daily *satsang*.

Practical suggestion No. 4 is, develop the spirit of detachment. Attend to your duties and be inwardly detached, knowing that nothing, nobody belongs to you. You are only an actor, and also a spectator, in the ever-unfolding, cosmic drama of life. You have to play this double role of an actor and a spectator. You do your duty, without considering what the other person is doing. We often say, so and so is not treating me properly: why must I be good to him? No, you must do your duty. In doing so, you will sow the right kind of *karma*.

When things do not work out the way we want them to, we feel frustrated. If, however, we work in the spirit of detachment, we shall remain unaffected. To work you have the right, says the Lord, but not to the fruit thereof. Work not for results but for the pure love of God: work as instruments in the Hands of the great Cosmic Power.

Practical suggestion No. 5 is, grow from more to more, in the spirit of surrender to God: "Not my will, but Thy Will be done, O Lord!" Repeat the Divine Name, and pray with a sincere heart that you may rise above the *dwandas*– the pairs of opposites, above pleasure and pain, loss and gain, for it is only then that suffering will not be able to touch us, and we shall be at peace with ourselves and with those around us.

Practical suggestion No. 6 is, be vigilant. Be watchful, live in awareness all the time. It was the Buddha who said to his disciples on one occasion: "*O bhikkhus*, if you are not vigilant, desire will enter your heart even as rain enters a room through a leaky roof."

Practical suggestion No. 7 is, do as much good as you can, to as many as you can, in as many ways as you can. Help as many as you can to lift the load on the rough road of life. The day on which we have not helped a brother here, a sister there, a bird here, an animal there is a lost day, indeed.

Question: "Can our bad *karma* be mitigated or lessened? Is there any hope for us?

Dada: Evil *karma* can be mitigated or lessened by *Nama-japa* and selfless service to those that suffer and are in pain and, above all, through the grace of God or a Godman.

Question: Can a human being reincarnate as an animal?

Dada: So let met repeat, the law of *karma* is not punitive but reformative. The law of *karma* is but one aspect of God. And God is love. Love would never wish to punish those it loves, but would always wish to see that they grow in perfection, from more to more. Therefore, *karma* puts us in an environment where we have opportunities to evolve spiritually and grow in perfection. If the law of *karma* feels that a particular human being, in the interest of his own evolution, needs to wear the body of an animal, the human being will reincarnate as an animal. Such a thing, however, is rare and occurs in cases where the life of a human being is worse than that of a brute beast.

It has been rightly said that no patient can prescribe for himself.

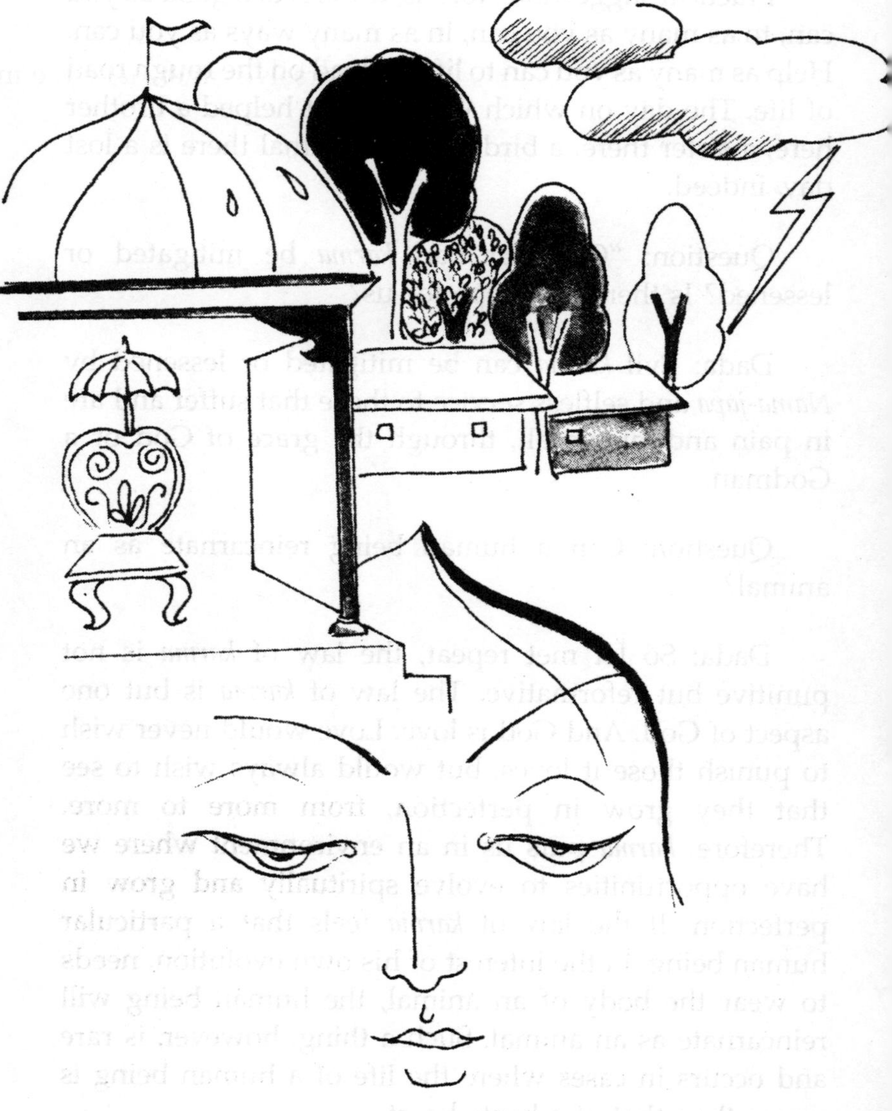

'Tis A Strange World!

It is a strange world in which we live, a world which is governed by the law of *karma*. A son is born to a father. He feels happy and rejoices. Little does he realise that the child has come to settle up old accounts.

A young man and his first cousin were in love with each other. After they got married, the girl found that her husband did not come up to her expectations. She asked for a divorce, and claimed from him the house in which they lived. Poor man, he had to surrender his house and is, today, wandering homeless!

Through *karma,* we come into contact with those with whom we have *karmic* involvements. We give them what we owe them and receive what they owe us.

Birth is never a matter of accident. *Karma* determines the family in which I am born. It is commonly believed that if I do evil, I shall be punished for it. The law of *karma,* however, is not punitive, but reformative. It may appear that the law of *karma* is punishing us for certain misdeeds we might have committed in the near or remote past. The law of *karma* never punishes. It puts us in an environment which may afford us opportunities for self-growth. The law of *karma* provides us with experiences meant to helps us to grow into better and nobler persons. Therefore, let us accept the situation in which we find ourselves and make the most of it by learning the lesson which a particular experience has come to teach us. That is the way of spiritual progress.

Karma binds those who identify themselves with their bodies (and the mind). *Karma* binds those who are conditioned by time and space. So many of us think: "I was born at such and such a time and at such and such a place. I am so many feet tall and weigh so many pounds. I am living in a palatial mansion and am prosperous and have great influence over the people." When we think along those lines, we create a cage of time and space within our own minds and stay cooped up in it all our life. In reality, we are not bound by time and space. It is we who have created time and space: time and space have not created us. "Birthless and deathless art thou, O Arjuna!" says the Lord in the *Gita*. "Weapons cannot wet thee, nor winds, dry thee away. Thou art immutable, eternal, all–pervading, beyond time and space."

Blessed is the person who realises the Self. For him there is no suffering. To him there are no problems. He has the freedom which belongs to the children of God. For us, children of time and space, there are seemingly endless problems. Man's greatest problem is himself– his own self.

Why Do Bad Things Happen To Good People?

Little Anita learnt to play on the harmonium. As she practised the same lesson, over and over, she felt bored and her fingers hurt. She complained to her teacher who said to her: "I know it hurts the fingers but it strengthens them, too." Then Anita packed the philosophy of the ages in her reply: "Teacher, it seems that everything that strengthens, hurts!"

Significant are the words of C. S. Lewis: "God whispers to us in our pleasures, speaks to us in our consciences, but shouts in our pains."

"Whom God loves, He smites!" sings a poet-saint of my native land. Whoever would be chosen of God must gladly submit to a process of purification. He must be prepared to pass through the fire of suffering and be purified as thrice-burnished gold. He must be found worthy of facing trials and tribulations, of courting dishonors and disgrace for the love of God.

There was a blacksmith who deeply loved God even though he had to face many a suffering and sickness. One of his acquaintances was an unbeliever. He said to him, one day: “How can you lay your trust in a God who sends suffering and sickness to you?”

Quietly answered the blacksmith: “When I have to make a tool, I take a piece of iron and put it into the fire. Then I strike it on the anvil to see if it will take temper. If it does, I know I can make something useful out of it. If not, I toss it on the scrap-heap. This has made me pray to the Lord, again and gain: “Lord! put me into the fire of suffering but, pray, do not throw me no the scrap-heap.”

In a passage of great beauty, the beloved poet of Sind, Shah Abdul Latif, says: “I have known of no one who met the beloved in happiness!” The Law of Love is the Law of the Cross, the Law of Sacrifice. Shah Latif sings:

They who embrace the Cross
And surrender their life breath,
To them is given the vision of God!

To the seeker after God, difficulties and dangers, trials and temptations come in an endless procession. He does not seek to run away from them.

The man who tries to escape trouble finds himself, sooner or later, in more serious trouble. Such is the law. No trial comes to us without a purpose. Every trial is a teacher (Guru): it comes to teach us a lesson we need to learn. Significant are the words of a Baul Song: "By what path comest thou, O Guru? The mystery I cannot solve!" And again:

The welcome you receive is your Guru!
The agony inflicted on you is your Guru!
Every hammer-blow on your heart is your Guru!
What makes you shed tears is your Guru!

We have so many lessons to learn and they differ from individual to individual. The lessons meant for me are not the lessons meant for you. Therefore, the trials God sends me are different from the trials He sends you.

Trials must not be resisted. To resist is to make strong. Do not resist trials, but welcome them. Everything that we welcome is transformed. Suffering is transformed into love. This is the great mystery of life.

Physical pain, mental agony, spiritual anguish, nothing lasts for ever. Everything lasts for as long as it has a purpose to fulfill. When it has done its work, it falls away like the dead, dry leaves of autumn.

Many are the problems and perplexities that a pilgrim has to face, as he treads the path. He knows that every one of them is necessary. He does not complain. He accepts difficulties as they come, makes them a part of his life, is nourished by them and moves a few steps nearer the goal.

There are periods when a pilgrim finds himself surrounded by utter darkness. He finds it difficult to welcome trials and temptations with enthusiasm. In no case must he avoid them. Deep within him is the faith that though the situation be exasperating, if only he will be patient and trusting, God will lead him out of danger into security, out of defeat into victory, out of darkness into Light!

The one practical way to meet a difficult situation is to walk right up to it, to look it in the face with courage and determination, and with the prayer: "So help me, God!" It is only when we are unwilling to meet a difficulty or are afraid to face it that it gets the better of us. When, trusting in God, we go forward to meet it, as we would meet a friend, the impossible happens. What was thought to be a trial, what appeared to be a source of danger and difficulty, is seen to be a blessing in disguise.

My thoughts go back to an incident which occurred in the days of my boyhood. It was a small incident to all appearance: but it taught me a lesson which I have not forgotten. It was the year 1925. I was a student in a Primary School: a private tutor taught me English at home. I asked a friend to give me a story book (in English) and he promised to bring it on the Holi Day.* The sacred day arrived. I heard a knock on the door. I eagerly moved forward to open it. The sight which greeted me was terrifying. There stood before me the fearful face of a lion. I screamed and ran into my home. Out of the lion's mouth issued words in a sweet, familiar voice: "Be not afraid! 'Tis I, Govind, thy dear friend! I have brought for thee the promised story book."

Immediately, fear vanished. I began to laugh. I moved forward to embrace my friend. I touched his face, which was covered with a mask. The fearful "lion's face" dropped down at a single touch, and my dear friend's face stood revealed. Ever since, I have tried to look at difficulties and dangers as friends who come to me wearing fearful masks, who always bring rich blessings.

* A sacred day in the calendar of India when people wear all types of masks.

Meet every difficulty bravely. Do not try to avoid it. You will find that difficulties are gifts which God sends us for the enrichment of our interior life. He is the Lord of Compassion and Love: and His works are ever the works of mercy. If only we trust Him and surrender ourselves to Him, asking Him to lead us wherever He will, fearing nothing, avoiding nothing, but rejoicing in all that He send us, no harm can ever come to us. And through every circumstance and situation will flow to us the love and joy and peace of God.

Fredrick Chopin, the great composer, had to struggle against an ailing body. Many a time he drew so close to death that news was frequently circulated that he had passed away. His friend, George Sand, addressed him as "My dear corps". And, in a humorous mood, Chopin once referred to his physicians' reports thus: "One said I would die, the second said I was about to die; the third said I was already dead!" Chopin attributed the charm of his music to suffering.

Of the great English poet, Longfellow, it is said that he was again and again tormented with neuralgia. He used to refer to it in the calmest and tenderest terms, sometimes saying: "The goddess Neuralgia, who compels me to stay in my loved home."

Fanny Crossby, the famous blind song-writer, was only six weeks old when a minor eye inflammation developed. The doctor, who treated her, was careless, and Fanny became totally blind. She harboured no bitterness against the physician. She made use of the tragedy to make her better instead of bitter. Referring to the physician on one occasion, she said: "If I could meet him now, I would say, thank you, over and over again, for making me blind." She felt blindness was God's gift to her, so she could write songs: and she has written more than 8,000 of them.

We must always find some reason or the other for which to feel thankful to God. If there is one thing which God loves, it is an humble, thankful heart. Even in the darkest hours of life, if only we turn around, we shall not fail to find something for which we have to feel thankful to God.

A friend of mine lost an eye in an accident. He was taken to a hospital. Several friends visited him and sympathised with him in his irreparable loss. They found him cheerful as ever. To them he said: "I thank God that one eye still remains. The accident could have robbed me of both the eyes: but God chose to protect one of them. Blessed be His Name!"

One of the most moving stories which Sadhu Vaswani told us is that of Bahram. He was a wealthy merchant. His caravans carried for sale in foreign lands, goods worth lakhs of rupees. One day, his caravans were looted by robbers. Bahram lost several lakhs.

One of his friends came to sympathise with him in his great loss. It was a time of famine. Bahram thought his friend had come in the hope of getting a meal. Bahram asked his servant to serve meals. The friend said: "I am not in need of a meal. I only came to sympathise with you in your loss.

And Bahram said: "It is kind of you to have come. But I am not worrying over what has happened. I feel grateful to God that though the robbers looted my goods, I have looted none! The robbers have not touched the Treasure Imperishable – the Treasure of faith in Allah, the Compassionate." It is the true Treasure of life!

O, Ye That Suffer!

People talk of God, but how many really *know* Him? We hear of God, we read concerning God, we speak about God, we visit temples and churches and sing songs in praise of God, but we do not know what God really is, for we have not yet had an experience of God. We have not seen Him: we have not spoken to Him: we have not heard His voice: we have not touched His Lotus Feet. Little wonder, an ever increasing number of young men and women today question the very existence of God. Many, indeed, echoing the words of Nistzsche, the great German thinker, declare: "God is dead!"

I recall a moving, little incident which occurred in Kerala, several years ago. At a meeting, a man, apparently a communist, got up and said: "All this talk about God is nonsense. There is no God! God is only a superstition created by some interested people to dupe the masses." Then he added: "If God really exists, let Him strike me dead within three minutes!" So saying, he held out a watch and kept on looking at it. The people heard the challenge being thrown in the face of God. The atmosphere of the meeting changed: it was charged with suspense. One minute passed: nothing happened! Two minutes...... two minutes and thirty seconds...... the people were tense...... two minutes, forty-five seconds...... two minutes, fifty seconds...... two minutes, fifty-five seconds...... two minutes, fifty-nine seconds, three minutes were over: the man continued to live! He triumphantly declared: "Did I not tell you, God is dead? A dead myth of dead past! If, as you say, an ominpotent God really existed, He would have struck me dead by now. He would have accepted my challenge. But God does not exist. All talk about God is mere humbug!"

At the meeting was present a simple man, a lover of God and a servant of suffering humanity, one who had dedicated his life to the Divine Spirit, one who, for the love of God, had become a homeless wanderer, moving from place to place, carrying to waiting multitudes the saving gospel of the love of God. He saw that the statement of the communist had profoundly affected the audience and thrown many of the people into confusion. He got up and said to them: "Do not for a moment believe that God does not exist. God exists! And God is Love! Even if you deny Him, His love continues to take care of you. He is our heavenly Father, more real and more loving than our earthly fathers. Which father amongst you would be prepared to strike his son dead, only to prove his existence? If your son threw a challenge at you, saying: "Father, if you really exist, slay me within three minutes, you would merely laugh at his foolishness."

Hearing this, a wave of joy spread over the meeting. The hearts of the listeners were filled with a new faith, and they declared with one voice: "God exists! All glory to Him!"

Is not God the Greatest Fact in history? I recall how, during the last century, a memorable dinner was held in London. A number of thinkers and scholars were present at the dinner. Dean Stanley was asked to preside and he proposed for discussion the topic: "Who will dominate the future?"

Prof. Huxley was the first to speak. In the course of his learned speech, he said: "The future will be dominated by the nation which sticks most closely to the facts." His speech created a deep impression on the minds of his hearers, who felt convinced that the future would be dominated by physical science and the material data furnished by it.

After a moment of silence, the dean called upon Edward Maill, Member of Parliament and President of the Royal Commission on Education. And this is what he said: "I have been listening to the last speaker with profound interest, and agree with him that the future will be dominated by the nation which sticks most closely to the facts. But I want to add one word. 'All' the facts! The greatest fact in history is God!"

Yes, the greatest fact in history is God. And true success belongs to those who work with God. During the days of the Civil war, Abraham Lincoln put a very pertinent question to his people. "It may be true", he said to them, "that God is on our side; but the real question is: Are *we* on the side of God?"

When the great English poet, Robert Louis Stevenson, sought spiritual illumination and found it, he wrote to his father: "No man can achieve success in life until he writes in the journal of his life the words, 'Enter God'!"

The question remains: "What is God? Can God be seen, contacted and talked to?" Those very questions haunted the mind of young Narendra (Swami Vivekananda), and he asked Sri Ramakrishna: "Have you seen God?" Quick came the reply from the saint: "Yes, I have seen God. I see Him more clearly than I see you!"

Narendra was not yet convinced. He asked: "Can I see God?"

"Yes," replied the Saint. "Everyone can see God!" Then, after a minute's silence, the saint said: "But where are they who are eager to see God? Men weep for women and women weep for men. Boys shed jugful of tears for girls and girls shed tears for boys. Where are they who shed tears in love and longing for the Lord? Verily, this I say to you, If you will but weep for the Lord with deep yearning in your heart, God will surely reveal Himself to you!"

We shed tears for the things which the world gives and the world takes away. We weep for our dear and near ones who belong to a world of transience. In this world nothing abides! Everything, every form, is as a bubble floating on the surface of water. One moment it is: another moment it has vanished! Alone God is! Blessed is the person whose heart is filled with pure love and longing for the Eternal Lord. A mark of this love is tears. When your eyes shed tears for the love of God, He is not from you afar. Just as the reddening of the skies at dawn is a sure sign that the sun is about to rise, even so the reddening of the eyes by tears of pure love and longing for His vision is a sure sign that the Lord will soon appear to you. Tears cleanse the stained mirror of the heart and enable you to behold the

Beauteous Face of the Beloved therein!

What is the shortest and easiest way to God? It is the way of complete self–surrender. And what is it to surrender? It is to give all you are and have to the Divine, knowing fully well that nothing, no one, belongs to you. It is to live for the love of God, not the self. It is to walk the way of obedience, to the Will Divine, to rejoice in all that happens, knowing that *everything* that happens is for our good. To surrender oneself is to hand oneself over completely, entirely, utterly to God.

There is a story of the little girl who went with her father to climb a mountain. At first, she wished to climb on her own. She said to her father: "Let me do it alone!" The father let her do it: she moved in front, and the father followed. She was glad to show to her father how strong and capable she was. In due course, the mountain grew steeper and more difficult to climb. She slipped and fell. The thorns pricked her feet and legs. Tears trickled down her cheeks. She would not give up. She had a strong will and was determined to show her father that she could do it all on her own. At last, the task became too difficult for her and, after the most cruel fall of all, she turned weeping to her father. He took her tenderly in his arms and reached her to the peak of the mountain.

We are like the little girl and will continue to suffer until we turn to the Father who is by us all the time, waiting for us to invite Him into our daily life. When we surrender ourselves to Him, He picks us up in His everlasting Arms and "reaches us to the peak of the mountain" where is Love and Joy and Peace.

We realise that we are not alone. One there is who is taking care of us. He is Omnipresent, Omnipotent, Omniscient. He looks after us. Our true security is at His Lotus Feet. Significant are the words of Sadhu Vaswani:

"The log doth not move: but the river can carry it to the other shore. Let but the log surrender itself to the river that flows.

"Krishna is the River that flows. Let but a man, no matter how burdened with sins, surrender himself to Him, and He will carry the devotee to the Other Shore!"

Let Every Day Be A Happy Day!

This morning, someone put to me a question: "What is meant by happy and blessed day?"

Every day comes to us as a gift out of the spotless Hands of God. Therefore, should every day be to us a happy and a blessed day. Alas! We spoil our days with our wild thinking and unholy living. We fill them with sorrows and sufferings which follow in the wake of a self–centred life.

I recall a beautiful, little story I read in the writings of a great *brahmagnani* of the West, the great German mystic Meister Eckhart.

There was a learned man who, for several years, longed to be shown the way to God. Every day, he sat apart from men and prayed that he might be brought into contact with a Sage, a Saint, a Knower or Truth.

One day, as he sat in prayer, he heard a voice say: "Go to such and such a place, and you will meet the man who will show you the way to blessedness and bliss!"

Great was his joy when he heard the words. Forthwith he went to the place indicated by the Voice. He was surprised to find a man, humble, simple, poor, with tattered clothes on his feet soiled with mud.

The learned man looked all around him, but found no other man seated there. So, to this man, he said: "Good morning to you!"

Quietly, answered the poor man: "I have never had a bad morning!"

"God give you good luck!" said the learned man.

"I have never had ill luck!" answered the poor man.

The learned man's astonishment grew. "May you be happy!" he said to the poor man.

To which the poor man answered: "I have never been unhappy!"

"I am unable to understand," said the learned man. "Pray, explain it all to me."

"Gladly," said the poor man. "You wished me a good morning. I have never had a bad morning. For, if I do not get food to eat, I praise God. If it rains or snows, or if the weather is foul, I still praise God. If I am despised and have no human company, I praise God! So I have never had a bad morning, never an evil day.

"You wished me good luck: but I have never had ill

luck. For I always dwell at the Lotus Feet of the Lord: and I know that whatever God sends to me is the very best that can ever happen to me. I cheerfully accept everything that comes to me – health or sickness, prosperity or adversity, joy or sorrow, as a gift from God. I have never had ill luck.

"You wished me happiness. I have never been unhappy. For the deepest longing of my heart is to live in union with God's Will, and I have so entirely yielded my will to the Will of God, that what God wills, I will!"

Astonished, the learned man asked: "What if God should will to cast you into hell?"

"Cast me into hell!" exclaimed the poor man. "God is too loving to do that. But, even if He sends me to hell, I should have two arms with which to embrace Him. One is the arm of humility, the other of love. With them, I should so embrace Him that He would have to go to hell with me. I would rather be in hell and be with God than be in heaven and remain away from God!"

The poor man taught that self-surrender, in utter humility, is the simplest, surest, nearest way to God.

When asked, who he was, he answered: "I am a king!"

He was the very picture of destitution: and yet he felt he was a king! For he had learnt to walk the way of acceptance. He accepted all that came his way and rejoiced in all that happened. He expected nothing: he hoped for nothing: he needed nothing: he lacked nothing. Was he not the richest of men on earth?

Of a simple, poor *dervish* it is said that a rich man wished to offer him some money– a thousand rupees. The *dervish* asked the rich man: "You are giving me a thousand rupees. How much do you have for yourself?"

"I have millions of rupees with me," said the rich man.

The *dervish* asked: "Do you still wish to have more?"

"Surely, yes!" answered the rich man.

"Then I shall not accept your thousand rupees," said the *dervish.* "For a rich man must not receive from one poorer than he!"

"But you have nothing," said the rich man. "How are you richer than I?"

The *dervish* answered: "Though I have nothing, I desire nothing. You have so much: still you desire more! Surely, the person who desires to have is poorer than the man who feels satisfied and desires nothing!"

Beautiful are the words ascribed to Jesus in a non-biblical saying: "Nothing in the morn have I, and nothing do I have at night. Yet, there is none on earth richer than I!" Jesus was the richest of men, for he desired nothing!

Such an one was the poor man in the story of Meister Eckhart. To him, everyday was a happy and blessed day! May it be the same with us!

We asked Sadhu Vaswani once: "When difficulties come, what do you do?"

"I praise the Lord!" was his answer.

We asked him again: "When you are ill and have suffering and pain, what do you do?"

He said: "I praise the Lord!"

We asked him again: "When you are in the midst of storm of life, what do you do?"

And he said: "Still I praise the Lord!"

In these few simple words is enshrined the secret of the truly happy and blessed life: "I praise the Lord!" May those four words be a *mantra* of our life! May we learn to praise the Lord in heat and cold, in joy and sorrow, in praise and censure, in pleasure and pain, in loss and gain – aye, in the face of disappointment, disaster, disease, death! Then, indeed, will we be proof against suffering and every day will be to us a happy and a blessed day!

'Tis Good To Do Good!

A student: Dada, what is the thought for today?

Dada: The thought for the day is: "The evil you do, remains with you: the good you do, comes back to you".

A word which was very dear to Sadhu Vaswani, was, "Give!" On one occasion, he said: "I have but one tongue. If I had a million tongues, with every one of those tongues, I would still utter the one word, give. To give is to live!"

How true it is that those that give, live. Those that give not are no better than dead souls.

Many of us, indeed, are dead souls, for we are not prepared to give. We feel happy to receive. In the world, there are two kinds of people: (1) those that give, and (2) those that receive. Let us belong to the first category. Let us give and give and give and never be tired of giving. Let us give without any thought of getting something in return. We must give freely, unconditionally. Conditional giving makes us shopkeepers. We go to a shop, give Rs. 10/- and, in return, get things worth Rs. 10/-. We must give, without expecting anything in return, not even a simple word of thanks.

Someone said to me: "I gave so much and in return received a scornful look!" Let us not give to the individual. Think of the individual as an image of God. You are giving to God. The individual is only a post-box. When you post a letter, do you think of the quality of the post-box? Whether it is new or old, well-maintained or otherwise? You just post the letter in the faith that it will reach the destination. One destination is God. Give in this spirit, and you will be abundantly blessed!

When I was in the school, we were told a story of a woman. She baked *chappatis* for the members of the family, and an extra *chappati* for a hungry passer-by. She kept the extra *chappati* on the window-sill, for whosoever would take it away. Every day, a hunchback came and took away the *chappati*. Instead of expressing gratitude, he muttered the following words before he went his way:

"The evil you do, remains with you:
The good you do, comes back to you!"

This went on, day after day. Everyday, the hunch back came, lifted, the *chappati*, and uttered the words:

"The evil you do, remains with you!"
The good you do, comes back to you:"

The woman felt irritated. "Not a word of gratitude," she said to herself. "But everyday this hunchback utters this jingo! What does he mean?"

One day, exasperated, she decided to do away with him. "I shall get rid of this hunchback," she said to herself. And what did she do? She added poison to the *chappati* she prepared for him! As she was about to keep it on the window-sill, her hands trembled. "What is this that I am doing?" she said to herself. Immediately, she threw the *chappati* into the fire and prepared another one and kept it on the window-sill. Sure enough, the hunchback came, picked up the *chappati* and muttered the words:

"The evil you do, remains with you:
The good you do, comes back to you!"

The hunchback proceeded on his way, blissfully unaware of the war raging in the mind of the woman.

Everyday, as the woman placed the *chappati* on the window-sill, she offered a prayer for her son who had gone abroad to seek his fortune. For many months she had no news of him. She prayed for the safe return of her son.

That evening, there was a knock on the door. As she opened it, she was surprised to find her son standing in the doorway. He had grown thin and lean. His garments were tattered and torn. He was hungry, starved and weak. Looking at his mother, he said: "Mother, it's a miracle that I have been able to reach you. When I was but a mile away, I was so famished that I collapsed. Just then, an old hunchback passed by. I begged of him for a morsel of food, and he was kind enough to give me a whole *chappati*. As he gave it to me, he said: "This is what I eat everyday: today I shall give it to you, for your need is greater than mine!"

As the mother heard those words, she turned pale. She leaned against the door for support. She remembered the poisoned *chappati* she had made that morning. Had she not hearkened to the voice of her conscience and burnt it in the fire, that *chappati* would have been eaten by her own son, and he would have lost his life. It was then that she realised the meaning of the hunchback's words:

"The evil you do, remains with you:
The good you do, comes back to you!"

A student: Dada tell us more!

Dada: Of Guru Nanak, we are told, that he gave a needle to a wealthy man and asked that it be returned to him in the heaven-world. The man agreed to do so. When he came home, he passed on the needle to his wife, saying: "Keep this needle safe with you. I have to return it to Guru Nanak when he meets me in the heaven-world."

"How can you do that!" the wife exclaimed. "Our own bodies we shall leave behind when we embark on the Great Journey. How can you carry this needle with you to the heaven-world?"

Yes, we can take nothing with ourselves, when we leave this world. Therefore, why not spend all we can in the service of those that suffer and are in pain?

A Student: Dada, it is said that the service you render

to others, returns to you at the right time and perhaps, ten-fold. Is that right?

Dada: I read an incident sometime ago concerning a Polish Air Force Pilot, Roman Tursky. He was flying his plane over Germany when the plane developed mechanical trouble and he made a forced landing on German soil. He sent his plane for repairs and spent the night in a hotel. The next morning, as he left his room, and was walking in the corridor, a little man came running and collided against him. Roman Tursky naturally felt offended. But, as he looked at the face of the little man, he found it pale with fright.

The man cried: "Gestapo! Gestapo!" Gestapo is the German secret Police. It was obvious that the man was being hounded by the Secret Police and he wanted to escape. Roman Tursky understood the situation and instantly pushed the man into his room, under his bed. Soon thereafter, the Police came in and interrogated Tursky. He did not understand their language, and the Police went away.

The Pilot offered to take this man to Warsaw where he was flying, but suggested that he get off a little before the plane reached the airport, as it was possible the police there would search his plane. So he dropped the man in a field a little before the plane reached the main airport. Sure enough, when he landed at Warsaw, the police was already there to make a search for the man.

Soon thereafter, there was the Second World War. Poland was occupied by Germany. Tursky flew to England and there joined the R.A.F., and became a war-hero. He was a brave man, and after destroying a number of enemy planes, his own plane was hit. It crash-landed.

The rescue party arrived there but found Tursky more dead than alive. He was shifted to the nearest hospital. The doctors despaired of him and hesitated to operate on him. The next day, newspapers flashed the news of Tursky's accident. Tursky was in a state of coma. However, when he recovered, he found a short man looking at him through bright eyes. "Do you remember me?" he asked Tursky. I was the one whom you saved. This morning, I read the news that you were in a state of coma, hanging between life and death, and immediately I flew here."

"What for?" asked Tursky.

"Because", the man answered, "I thought I might be of help. They say that I am one of the best brain surgeons. I came here, performed the operation, which has saved your precious life."

When you do good, remember that good will return to you. The evil you do, remains with you!

How To Overcome Trouble

At the heart of everyone, everything, is goodness. And this is true of every experience, howsoever unpleasant it may appear to be. Life is a mixture of the "pleasant" and the "unpleasant", of joy and sorrow. As the great English poet, William Blake, says in one of his poems: "Joy and woe are woven fine, a clothing for the soul divine!" And as the Psalmist declares: "Weeping may endure for a night, but joy cometh in the morning!" Joy and sorrow follow each other as day follows night. But when suffering comes, the period of tribulation appears to be interminably long. A year of joy is but as a day: and a day of suffering appears longer than a year.

Suffering is a part of life, and suffering is a teacher. We would miss some of the best lessons of life, if suffering did not come to us. Many of us, alas! do not recognise this truth and do all we can to avoid a seemingly painful experience. When trouble approaches, we try to run away from it: but trouble can never be dodged. The unpleasant experience recedes, only for a

while, to return to us again, wearing a more formidable form. By avoiding trouble, we invite greater trouble, at a later stage.

There are some who, knowing that trouble cannot be avoided, resign themselves to the experiences which fall to their lot. They do not resist: they become resigned. Often times, such persons are heard to say: "What cannot be cured must be endured!"

But there is a third way of meeting trouble, it is the only right way. The first way, the way of avoiding trouble, is folly. The second, the way of becoming resigned, is *avidya,* ignorance. The third is the way of greeting every unpleasant experience as a friend. Do not try to run away from trouble: you cannot do it. Do not let in trouble, simply because you must. But move forward to met trouble, to greet it with the words: "Welcome, friend! What message do you bring to me from God?" And you will find that every trouble is a soiled packet, soiled on the outside, but which contains a precious gift. Every unpleasant experience is a package which hides a wealth of wisdom and strength. The person, who knows this, greets suffering with a smile. He is a true victor, and his way is the way of victory.

Of one such man, I read some years ago. He had a flourishing business. Suddenly, one night, when he was away from town, his shop and house caught fire, and all that he possessed was reduced to ashes. His property of several lakhs were lost. What did he do? Shed tears? No! On his face was a smile, and lifting up his eyes, he asked: "Lord! What wouldst Thou have me do next?" And over the shambles, which once was his shop, he put up a signboard on which were the following words:

Shop burnt!
House burnt!
Goods burnt!
But faith not burnt!
Starting business tomorrow!

Here was a man who knew of the right way to meet trouble.

Are You Aware You Have An Unseen Friend?

Not long ago, a sister came to me. Her eyes were touched with tears. She sobbed as she spoke. Her husband, whom she loved and who loved her, had decided to travel to a distant land for purposes of business. He did not lack money: God had given him plenty of it. "He does not need to go so far, leaving me here all alone," she said. "Pray that he may abandon the idea altogether,"

My answer might have appeared cruel to her at that time. "I do not pray for this or that to happen," I said to her. "I shall pray that you may grow into an understanding of what God wills for you and that you may co-operate with His Will and let it work, uninterrupted, in and through you!"

The day arrived when she bade her husband a tearful good-bye. "You did not do anything for me," she said to me." You could have helped me, if only you had wished

to do so!"

I smiled and said: "Sister! Do not despair! God fulfills Himself in many ways!"

After a few months, she met me again. Her face was wreathed in smiles. "Now I know," she said "that there is the Hand of Divine Love and Wisdom in all that happens. When my husband left, I wept and wept. Then, gradually, it dawned on me that if God had willed my dear one to travel to a far country, it must all be for my good. Indeed, it has proved to be so. My husband's going away has given me many spare hours, I utilise them in a study of the *Gita* and the *Guru Granth Sahib* and Sadhu Vaswani's beautiful books on the *Santbani* and the lives of Saints. I pray and I meditate. I sit in Sadhu Vaswani's holy company. I sing God's Name and I serve the children of the poor and the lowly. They love me: I love them. And I feel happy and blessed!"

This is perfectly true. Our Journey through life has been perfectly planned by Infinite Love and Infinite Wisdom: there can be no mistake. Every experience that comes to us is just the right experience occurring at the right time to train us in the right way. So, let us accept all that comes and never attempt to circumvent anything.

Again and again, we try to run away from what appears to us as unpleasant experiences: again and again, we try to avoid what we regard as difficult situations. We may succeed in keeping them away for a while, but we can never avoid them all the time, for they are, indeed, essential to our growth. God means us to face them and so to develop our moral and spiritual muscles. If we avoid an unpleasant experience, it will return to us in due course with redoubled force, and we shall be compelled to take up the challenge until we have learnt the lesson it has come to teach us. The best way, therefore, to face difficult situations is to accept them and co-operate with their inner purpose, all the while fixing our mind and heart on Him who has planned for each one of us the glorious liberty that belongs to the children of the Spirit.

He whose refuge is the Lord lives in the constant awareness of God's presence. Such a man is never alone! Another is always with him, by him, guiding him, protecting him, leading him on! He hears His gentle footfalls: he feels the warm pressure of His Hand on his: he hearkens to the voice of his Unseen Friend: and he always feels safe and secure even in the face of danger and death.

How To Overcome Desire

Life is a battle-field. To face the battle of life, we need the strength of the Spirit. It is more important than the strength of the body. The Rishis of India named it *atma shakti*, the power of the Spirit. He who has it, is able to face the foe with ease and grace.

What is the foe of man? Desire, says the *Gita*, is the deadliest foe of man. Therefore, conquer desire! Conquer craving! The cause of so much of our suffering is desire. The great teacher of wisdom, Hermes, said: "If a man holds aloof from the desires of this world, the misfortunes of this world hold aloof from him."

Desires are of different types. And different desires overwhelm man at different times. So it is that Confucius said: "When young beware of fighting; when strong, beware of sex; and when old, beware of possessions."

Sri Ramakrishna repeatedly urged that the seeker on the path must keep clear of two desires – the desire for *kamini* and *kanchan*, lust of the flesh, and greed of gold.

Sadhu Vaswani asked us to refrain, in addition, from the desire for power, the desire to grow great or famous. For power, too is a lust. As the great English poet, Shelley, says: "Power, like a desolating pestilence, pollutes whatever it touches." The truly spiritual man is free from desires. "Be desireless!" says the *Gita*. What is the mark of him who has become desireless? In the words of the *Upanishad,* such an one looks with equal eyes upon a poisonous snake or a garland of flowers, a strong enemy or a kind friend, a costly jewel or a lump of earth, a bed of flowers or a slab of a stone, a group of beautiful women or useless straw.

Bayazid al–Bistami was one such man. "God delivered me from the desire for women to such a point," he said "that I cannot tell, when a woman appears to me, whether it is a woman or a wall." Fu Hsuan, the Chinese mystic, was another such man. "Though gold and gems by the world are sought and prized," he exclaimed, "to me they seem no more than weeds or chaff!"

Of Jesus it is said, that one day, he struck the ground with his hand and took some of it and spread it out, and behold, he had gold in one of his hands and clay in the other. Then turning to his companions, he asked: "Which of the two is sweeter to your hearts?" They said: "Gold." But Jesus said: "They are both alike to me." To him who is desireless, gold and clay are alike.

There is a story of a husband and his wife who both renounced the world and went out on a pilgrimage to various shrines.

One day, as they were moving on, the husband, who was a little ahead of the wife, saw a sparkling diamond on the ground. Immediately, he covered it with a handful of mud, thinking that, if his wife saw it, she might perchance be moved by greed and thus lose sight of the great ideal renunciation.

While he was thus busy, the wife came up and asked him what he was doing? The husband gave an evasive reply. She noticed the diamond, however, and reading his thoughts, said to him: "Why did you renounce the world, if you still feel the difference between the diamond and the dust?"

The practical problem is, how to achieve the state of desirelessness. Different answers to this question have been given by different teachers. Sadhu vaswani said to us: "To become desireless, sing the Name of God and give the service of love to all who suffer and are in pain."

Sri Ramakrishna said: "God cannot be seen so long as there is the slightest taint of desire; therefore have thy small desires satisfied, and renounce the big desires by right reasoning and discrimination."

The great *Sufi* teacher, Niffari, said: "Consider the last of everything if, thou wilt depart from the dream of it." In the *Srimad Bhagavatam*, we are told: "When one sees this Universe as ephemeral, one gains true discrimination and turns away from worldliness. The Self becomes the Saviour of self."

The great teacher of our days, Sri Ramana Maharishi, said: "Every time you attempt satisfaction of a desire, the knowledge comes that it is better to resist. Repeated reminders of this kind will, in due course, weaken the desire."

Let us follow what method we will. The goal of being

desireless must always be in front of us. As the *Upanishad* says: "Arise! Awake! Stop not until the goal is reached!"

Count Your Blessings

There are two types of people: First, there are those who will always count their blessings. Howsoever dark the night, howsoever stormy the weather, howsoever difficult the situation they find themselves in, they will lift up their hearts in gratitude to God: they will count their blessings. The second is the type of people who will forget the favours they have received from God and from those around them and will start complaining. Their complaints are endless.

Researches have been made by psychiatrists at Duke University Medical Centre in the U.S.A. The researches reveal that those that have a complaining nature have five times the level of heart diseases than those that count their blessings and give thanks. The complainers are likely to have clogged arteries. Therefore, even in the interest of your health, make this a rule of your life: Always count your blessings: count them one by one!

There was a man, a disgruntled person, who always complained about everything: he was an unhappy man. He felt unwanted and rejected and was resentful. The same man, today, is cheerful, optimistic, sunny and bright. When asked what brought about the change in his life, he said: "I owe it all to one magic word, "Thanks". "There was a time," he explained, "when the world, "thanks", did not exist in my dictionary." Today, he keeps on thanking everyone for every little thing that is done for him. "When you thank someone for doing something for you," he said, "you feel happy and the other person feels happy. Therefore, keep on thanking everyone. Above all, thank the Lord!"

Always count your blessings: count them one by one!

There is a story of two people who were shipwrecked. They found themselves on an island, which was uninhabited. Out of branches and leaves of trees, they built a cottage.

One of the two men was a complainer: the other was a thanker, one who counted his blessings. The first one kept on complaining: there was no end to his complaints. The second one said: "We still have so much to be grateful for. We are on solid earth: we could have been drowned. We have hands with which we can work and feet with which we walk. We have eyes with which we can see. Thank You, God! Thank You, God! Thank You, God!"

Everyday, both of them would go out to the seashore and wave their hands or handkerchiefs, in the hope that some passing steamer would view them from afar, and come to their rescue. Every evening, they returned to their cottage.

One evening, as they returned, they found that the cottage had caught fire and been reduced to ashes. The

complainer cursed the elements. The other man said to him: "Friend, be not depressed. Surely, there must be some good in this, too! God must have meant well by us! Thank You, God! Thank You, God!" The complainer felt exasperated and shouted: "You and your God! I shall have nothing to do with both!"

However, the next morning, as they went to the seashore, they found a small steamer waiting for them. The captain of the boat explained that the previous day he had seen smoke rising from the island which made him feel that there were some who might need his help. Involuntarily, out of the lips of the thanker came the words: "Thank You, God! Thank You, God!" For the first time, the complainer also said: "Thank You, God! Thank You, God!"

May we always count our blessings: count them one by one. Some days ago, I went to a Hospital. They took me to a man who suffered from depression. He looked perfectly healthy but was depressed.

I gave him a few sheets of papers and a ball-pen and asked him to write down all the things for which he felt he should feel grateful to God. "Feel grateful to God, for what?" he asked in surprise. I said to him: "There are so many blessings you have received. You have parents who love you. You have friends who come and visit you. You are above need. You have an able body, if you think of them, you will find there are a thousand things for which you should feel grateful to God! List them all on those sheets of paper and on every sheet write, "Thank You, God! Thank You, God!" Two days later, they found that the young man did not need any treatment. He was perfectly all right. He walked out of the Hospital even before he could get a discharge.

There is the therapy of thanksgiving. Let us keep on thanking everyone for every little thing they do for us. Above all, let the words be on our lips all the time: "Thank You, God! Thank You, God! Thank You, God!" And depression will not draw nigh unto us, and we will be happy as waves dancing on the sea.

Four Steps To Serenity

Silence is our true teacher. Silence is our real Guru! In silence are all our doubts cleared. And in silence is heard the Voice of God which speaketh the ancient word: *Uttishtha! Jagrata!* O sleeper, Arise! Awake! How long will you in slumber lie?

To awake is to know that we are not creatures of the earth, earthy. We do not belong to this world. Our Home, whence we are come and whither we must return, is beyond the pathways of planets and stars. So we must live in the world but not be of the world. It was Sri Ramakrishna who said: "Live in the world but keep the pitcher steady on your head: that is to say, keep the mind firmly on God."

Yes, we must attend to our daily tasks but our mind should be fixed on the Lotus Feet of the Lord. We must practise the presence of God. And He is not afar. He is with us, within us. Nearer is He to us than the nip of our neck, closer is He to us than breathing.

To practise the presence of God, elaborate rites and ceremonies are not needed. What is needed is love and

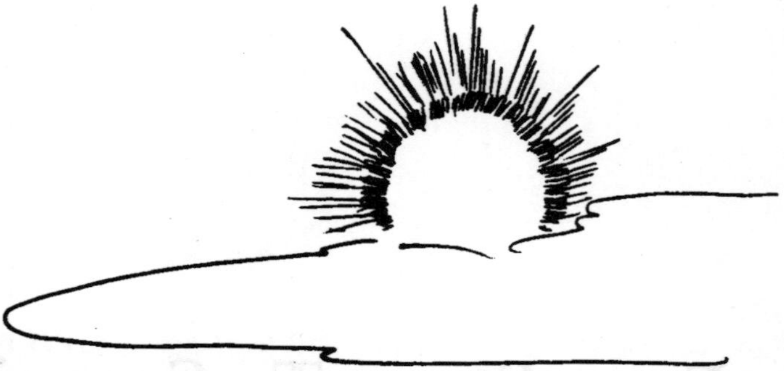

childlike trust. Let us go to God as a child would go to its mother or father. Let us place all our problems and needs before Him. In Him is the solution to all our problems: and in Him is all that we need!

To practise the presence of God, (1) Let us continually converse with Him. He is the Beloved of our hearts. He is the Friend among friends. Let us speak to Him, again and again. Let us whisper to Him words of love. Let us express gratitude to Him for the blessings He has bestowed upon us. Let us speak to Him with intimacy and familiarity.

(2) Let us have faith in him, faith that whatever He does is for our good. For His works are ever the works of mercy.

(3) Therefore, let us abide in the Will of God. Let this be the one prayer of our heart: "In sun and rain, in pleasure and pain, in loss and gain, Thy Will be done!"

And (4) Let us be ever watchful, ever vigilant. For passions wake up in the heart of man, again and again. And they lead him astray: they take him miles away from the Beloved of the Heart.

The Perfect Man

The ideal of every true seeker of God should be perfection. Each one of us should strive to be perfect. It was Jesus who said: "Be ye perfect, even as your Father in Heaven is perfect!" Even as God is perfect, even so must we aspire after perfection. The perfect man, by the Sufis, is called, *"kaamil–e–insaan"*. Let each one of us strive to be perfect.

What is the mark of a perfect man? This, that he wanders not. How much do we not wander! It may appear that we are seated in one place: but our minds keep on wandering. "What is the quickest, the fastest thing in the world?" a sage was asked. And he answered: "The mind." See how fast the mind travels, faster than sound, faster than a Concord. One moment it is here: another moment it is in New York: a third moment it is in Taiwan. The mind keeps on wandering: the mind will never be still.

As the mind wanders, we keep on wandering with it. Our bodies may be in one place. But our thoughts are scattered. They keep moving from one place to another, one object to another, one form to another. Suppose I were to ask you to keep your minds fixed on one object, one idea, just for one single minute, how many of you would be able to do that? Can you keep your minds still just for half a minute? I shall give you half a minute (½ a minute's silence). Tell me if during that brief, very brief period, the mind of anyone of you was still? If you will be sincere, you will tell me that, even in the brief space of half a minute, your minds kept on wandering.

The perfect man is one whose wandering has ceased. Like us, he has passed through many experiences. He has suffered: he has shed tears: he has offered prayers: he has attended *satsangs*. He has been crushed by the grinding wheels of the mill of *maya*. At last, his soul has ripened and he has become perfect. His wandering hath ceased. He wandereth no more.

Men suffer because they wander. The cause of their wandering is three-fold. *Maya* has three faces, three prongs.

(1) The first is pleasure, sense gratification. See how pleasure draws us. The cinema, the theatre, the club, the disco, the snack bar, all these and so many other things fascinate us, wake up within us desires. It is desires that make us wander. Right now many of us have so many desires: though we are sitting here, we are wandering after our desires. The whole world is running after, dancing to the tune of desires. This dance of desires is the dance of death. If you would be perfect, keep away from desires. Control desires: do not let desires control you!

(2) The second face, the second prong of *maya* is wealth. See how people run after wealth. They keep on

amassing more and more wealth. They do not have the time to spend it! Suddenly, death pounces upon them and, leaving their millions behind, they move on empty-handed to the Other Shore.

(3) The third face of *maya* is name, fame, earthly greatness. There are people who shun pleasures, who keep away from wealth, but who want name and fame, popularity and publicity. They want the applause of the people. They, too, are prisoners of *maya* and do not attain to perfection.

O ye, who would wish to be perfect, keep away from these three snares – pleasure, wealth, power. Sing the Holy Name of God. Sing it, again and again, with love and longing of the heart, with tears in your eyes, and give the service of love to those that suffer and are in pain, and you, too, will grow in perfection and you, too, will be filled with *ananda*, the bliss that no ending knows!

Welcome Suffering!

A holy woman tells us that the Lord appeared to her, one day, and said: "I bring to you three gifts: choose the one you like most!"

The three gifts were — undeserved criticism, disease and persecution.

The saint weighed the three gifts and found that each was more difficult than the remaining two. "To be criticised for no fault of mine! To be called a bad character, a thief, a liar, a hypocrite, when I am innocent.......?" "To become a victim to disease, to lie in bed, unable to move, unable to get up, perhaps unable to speak, and be in this condition month after month, year after year.......?" "To be treated as a criminal when my life is spotless, to be persecuted, flogged, terribly tortured.......?"

All the three seemed unbearable, and she trembled as she thought of what would happen if she chose any of those three gifts.

The Lord smiled and, in His extended hand, were

the three gifts. As she looked up into His tender, smiling face, something happened to her and, unhesitatingly, she said: "Lord, I take all the three!"

A holy man who, for many years, was active in the service of God and His suffering children, said with candid simplicity: "Lord, You have cheated me! When I offered myself to Your service, I felt that all I would receive would be tears, hunger, starvation, perspiration, vexation, oppression, persecution, pain. But You have given me the sweetest comfort. I feel cheated, Lord! But it is a happy misunderstanding."

Those that offer themselves to the service of God are out for many surprises. Their life is truly a life of adventure. Kagawa lay in a hospital, threatened with total blindness. He spent many months in a dark room with thick bandages covering his eyes. When they said to him: "Your health is gone: your sight is gone. Are you not afraid of approaching death?" He calmly answered that there was nothing he feared in this wide, wonderful, God-filled world."

"As I lie in this dark room," he said, "God still gives light. Pains that pierce the very fires of Hell itself sweep over me. Yet, even in the melting fires of Hell, God's mercy, for which all of earth's manifold treasures would be an utterly inadequate exchange, still enfolds me."

"To me all things are vocal," he continued. "Oh, wonder words of love! The bedding, the tears, the spittle, the perspiration, the vapour of the compress on my eyes, the ceiling, the matted floor, the voice of the chirping sparrow without, all are vocal. God and every inanimate thing speak to me. Thus, even in the dark I feel no sense of loneliness."

It was an early hour of the morning. The first flutings of birds had died, and many of them, with wings outstretched, were flying in the skies. Hundreds of little doves were lazily sitting on the terrace, cooing to each other, awaiting their morning meal. In our small garden, flowers smiled and green leaves of shrubs and trees glistened in the first rays of the morning sun. All nature appeared gray, beautiful as a bride on her wedding day. But my heart was sad.

Sadhu Vaswani lay ill, in great pain. He had passed a restless night: and though his eyelids were heavy with sleep, the shooting pains all over his body would not let him sleep for over a minute or two at a time. I had watched him throughout the night and had seen how even when the pain was very acute, he continued to smile. When the pain became unbearable, out of his parted lips came but one word: *"Shukur! Shukur!"* Gratitude to thee, O Lord of Mercy!"

His feeble body was so broken with illness and pain that it was a wonder how he could bear it. I, also wondered that this prince amongst men, this man of singular purity and prayer, service and sacrifice, who would not hurt an ant, and who gave the love of his gentle, generous heart to all, the rich and the poor, the young and the old, the sinner and the saint, and who loved birds and animals and every flower of the field and every lotus in the lake and every atom of matter and every ray of light, I wondered that such a man should have to suffer so terribly.

Through Sadhu Vaswani healing had flowed to many

who were sick and afflicted. Now, when he was in the throes of pain, nothing could be done to give him relief! The doctor were helpless. We, who were near him, could only wake and watch and shed hidden tears of sorrow. But all the while he rejoiced in his heart that, by making him endure great agony of body, God was using him to give healing to others. I recalled how it was said of Jesus in the long ago: "He saved others: Himself He cannot save!" Such is the way of those who would be the saviours and servers, the helpers and healers of humanity!

At about three o'clock in the night, finding it difficult to bear the sight of this suffering, I said to him: "Beloved! You are a friend of God. Why will you not pray to Him that He may heal you of this illness which your feeble body is unable to bear? Surely God will listen to your prayers!"

Quietly, he answered: "To me, my child! there is nothing sweeter than the Will of the Lord. And if it be His Will that I suffer, such suffering is sweeter to me than relief from pain: for, verily, in the fulfillment of His Holy Will is my real comfort and solace!" After a brief while, with uplifted eyes, he prayed: "Gratitude to Thee, my God and my Lord! for this gift of pain. And if it be Thine Will to add to it tenfold, I pray Thee to do so without delay. In Thy Will alone is the peace I seek!"

I recalled how the great woman-mystic, Rabia, being urged by a friend to pray for relief from illness, answered: "Do you not know who it is that wills this suffering for me? Is it not God who wills it? Why, then do you bid me ask for what is contrary to His Will? It is not well to oppose one's Beloved."

With the first streaks of the dawn, Sadhu Vaswani's pain showed signs of abatement. When morning came, he met brothers and sisters, some of whom had travelled long distances to come and see him. One, who came from Bombay, on seeing him, exclaimed: "Why do the saints of God suffer?"

And he answered: "It is only the body that suffers."

Some one asked: "O saint of God! You have often spoken to us of the Law. And the Law, you say, is just. But what is our experience? There is anything but justice in this world where the innocent ones suffer and the wicked flourish as a bay-tree. So many who live good, pure lives and remember God, again and again, do not get enough to eat. While many others, who live a life of sensual enjoyment, go to the cinema house and the club, and drink and gamble and are forgetful of God, have huge bank balances. The devotees of God are afflicted with sorrow and sickness. The unbelieving ones are blessed with health and wealth and power and authority. Surely, such a sorry scheme of things cannot bear testimony to the operation of a law which is either just or merciful."

For a brief moment, Sadhu Vaswani was silent: A smile played upon his lips and a radiance shone in his eyes. And he said:

"What you say would be true if this earthly existence were the beginning and the ending of life. This finite physical existence of which we are conscious is but one stage in the journey of life. From eternity we come: to eternity we go. When our earth-pilgrimage is over, we shall continue elsewhere. And, if we have grown in true knowledge, we may then understand a little of what

appears to us today as enigmatic."

Then, pointing to the stump of a tree in the garden, he said:

"Beneath the strokes of a woodcutter's axe I saw that tree fall, several months ago. What must have been the feelings of the tree as blow after cruel blow fell on it? Perhaps the tree knows better now. Out of its wood have been fashioned doors and windows which protect many a poor man from the onslaught of rain and storm. The tree may know today that the agony through which it passed was part of a plan.

"What gives to the Saints their healing power? What makes the men of God redeemers of their race? This, that they receive the arrows of pain as gifts from the All–Giver! Alike in sunshine and in rain, they rejoice and give gratitude to God and sing His Holy Name. Every great one of Humanity has had to bear his cross. Krishna and Buddha and Jesus walked through the valley of the shadow of death. Who are we to say: 'We must escape sorrow, anguish, pain?' We, too, must bear our cross, bear and bleed.

"And when we bleed, let us remember that the Will of God is working through us: and through suffering and pain, God's Will is purifying us, preparing us for the vision of the One Lord of Life and Light and Love in all that is around us, above us, below us, within us.

"Suffering is the benediction which God pours upon His beloved children to whom He would reveal the meaning of His infinite mercy, reveal Himself, His Wisdom and His Love!"

And one said: "Yet, how natural it is for us, to try to get over sorrow!"

And our beloved Master said:

"That is so, my child! Because we still are creatures of the flesh. The flesh cries to get *over* sorrow: but the soul cries to get *into* sorrow and at the heart of it greet her God!

"In the dark abyss is water found: and the water of life may be found in the dark abyss of sorrow.

"The light of the sun is dimmed by the passing clouds: and when the clouds have moved on, the sun shines all the brighter. So the pure man becomes all the more radiant after the clouds of sorrow have passed over him."

And I said: "Beloved! Tell us more. To hear you is to bathe in the purifying waters of the Ganges, is to be filled with new aspirations for the true life – the life that is life, indeed."

And the master said:

"I know not much. I only know that there is suffering in the world. And men and women wander in darkness. In such a world let me go about giving love and compassion to all. Let me serve the poor and broken ones, serve my brothers and sisters, serve birds and beasts and all creatures in whom is the breath of life. Let me not waste energy in questions or controversies. Let me light a few candles at the altar of suffering creation.

"If I meet a hungry man, let me not ask why he is hungry, when so many others feast at their banquet tables. Let me give him food to eat.

"If I meet a naked man, let me not ask why he shivers in the cold of wintry nights, when so many have their wardrobes filled to overflowing. Let me give him garments to wear.

"And if I meet a man lost in sin, let me not ask why he is lost, but with a look of compassion, with a song or a syllable of love, let me draw the sinner to the spirit.

"Let me draw by awakening the longing that lies latent in all.

"Let me lead some out of darkness into light!"

Three Ways To Face Suffering

She was a sweet child of God. She had been bed-ridden for many months. At times, her pain became so excruciating that, were it not for her faith in God, she would want to shoot herself. In spite of this, there was a beautiful smile on her face. And out of her parted lips the words came, again and again: "O Lord! This, too, is for my good! Blessed be Thy Name!"

It was my privilege to be of some little service to her, from time to time. She bore all the suffering in the true heroic spirit. She was a girl of deep, abiding faith in God. Many came to her for blessings: she blessed them all. She prayed for them, for she believed profoundly in the power of prayer. It was said that her prayers were always answered.

I found her, one day, in the throes of physical agony. I said to her: "Why do you not pray to God to cure you? He will surely answer your payers!"

She smiled as she said that there were three important